H. J. Long

SOME PREACHERS DO!

SOME PREACHERS DO!

By BERTIE COLE BAYS

THE JUDSON PRESS

CHICAGO • PHILADELPHIA • LOS ANGELES

PRINTED IN THE U.S.A.

To my husband who in no way en-
couraged the writing of this book; but
who endeavored to suppress it by
threat and bribe!

Drawings by Calvin E. Ervin

Introduction

When the volume *Some Preachers Do!* came into my possession, it was read with consuming delight. The author's humorous sarcasm, the expert knowledge of ministerial secrets, and the truly vivid portraits of idiosyncrasies attached to every pastor's life, proved to be captivating.

Everyone is looking for firsthand information. This is indeed true of us preachers. We are called upon to participate in so many varied activities, and find ourselves involved in so many different situations, that we are quite anxious to know, not only how our environment looks, but how we ourselves react to it.

The author of this volume, out of very close observation and intimate understanding, has set forth beautifully for us a very true picture, in colors as varied as those of a rainbow. She has painted the portrait of ministers in almost every situation, so that one does not have to draw on his imagination, but can vividly see just what happens.

Every preacher, whether he needs it or not, ought to read *Some Preachers Do!* If he doesn't need it, he will find it filled with actual experiences of a minister's life portrayed in unforgettable colors. If he does need it, he will discover some of the many pitfalls that await the pilgrimage of every man of God.

The author has rendered a very valuable service to every

minister in the writing of this volume, for in it he has the opportunity of seeing the "don'ts" as well as the "do's." I should like to commend this book, not only to the reading of every minister but, also, to his parishioners. It will delight both pulpit and pew, and the rewards are great to those who honestly and faithfully read and observe.

GEORGE W. WISE

CONTENTS

TABLE OF ILLUSTRATIONS

Foreword

Oswald B. Boloni,
Wheat City, Kansas

My dear Oswald:

Your mother, Emma Alice, writes me that you have decided to enter the ministry. It seems to me that there are many things that I, out of my wide experience, should tell you. Perhaps you can profit by these remarks.

A preacher, Oswald, is a good mixer equipped with a loud-speaker, a streamlined body, the thick skin of a mule, the patience of God, a bottle of oil, and a can of Flit.

He is employed by an organized group of Christian people to preach two or three sermons on Sunday, to conduct a midweek service, to marry their children and to bury their dead; to encourage, to advise, to uplift, to warn, to lead and to love them; to pray for them; and to stand by as the last breath leaves the body of a loved one. Besides these duties, he must be an all-round businessman and executive, so that the affairs of the church may move smoothly and wax prosperous.

Now a minister has no boss and so does not work by rules and regulations. He can please himself, provided he does not displease some two or three hundred, or seven or eight hundred, more or less, members of his congregation. He can plan his work to suit himself, pray when he chooses, study when he chooses — of course, subject to constant interruption and demand that he go here and there and do this and that (Did he find Mrs. Jones's purse in the church? If not, will he please go and look and call Mrs. Jones's daughter?). In returning to his sermon, he may find six men with six grievances lined up at his study door. A minister's time is his own! So in order that you may use your time wisely, and avoid certain pitfalls and mistakes, and become a figure in your denomination, I am going to give you some advice concerning the work of the ministry, ministerial etiquette, and your position in general.

You will have the poorest material of any profession on earth with which to work. The contractor can demand the best of materials; the physician, the purest of drugs; the jeweler, the most flawless of stones; but the minister, working with human nature, finds so much bad in the best and so much unexpected good in the worst, that the structure which he builds is so amazing a combination of weakness and of strength, of solid timber and of worm-eaten boards, of beauty and of hideous hypocrisy, that God alone can distinguish the maze, trace the pattern, and call it "good" or "bad."

Cal decided to draw you some pictures. He didn't know just how to make them until he went to a preachers' convention and noted that most of the preachers seemed to be bald-headed and fat. So in order that no one's feelings may be hurt, he will draw them tall and thin with lots of hair. We hope you like the pictures and that our advice will be really helpful.

Your loving,

AUNT B.

SOME PREACHERS DO!

1

How to Get a Church

A preacher without a church is like ham without eggs, or Noah without the ark, or a sandwich without the filling, or a vest without a pair of pants. So the first step in becoming pastor of a church, Oswald, is to get the church.

Before coming to the decision that you must have a church, certain things will be true. You will have felt a call to preach from:

(1) God, (2) your family (in your case, your mother), (3) yourself.

Some, Oswald, are in the ministry by accident; some have it thrust upon them by fond mothers; and with others like the makings for hash, it just accumulates. From our own observation, Oswald, we advise that you do not preach unless God has called you to do so. Self-made men may make a success of it, but self-made preachers never do. The self-made preacher has the wrong perspective, the wrong motive, the wrong ambition, and the wrong sense of values. By his horn ye shall know him. His favorite verse is "Toot your own horn, or verily it shall not be tooted."

It may be that you have called yourself into the ministry through certain desires of your own heart, reasoning thus: "The minister goes in the best of company. He is looked up to and admired. He is often in the presence of agreeable and attractive ladies. He is not compelled to do manual labor and to wear the toil-stained clothing of the workingman. His life is easy and pleasant." If your reasoning runs in this fashion, and your "call" consists of the urge of your own desires, remember that you go in your own strength to face:

1) The preparation of some two hundred sermons and addresses for each year; 2) numerous funerals of all descriptions; 3) domestic cases in which you sit as judge and mediator; 4) poverty; 5) persecution; 6) opposition; 7) popularity on one hand and criticism on the other; 8) sacrifice; 9) self-denial; 10) dying men who need strength and comfort and Jesus Christ; and 11) sin-sick souls who come to confess and to find peace.

If you think you can do all these things in your own strength, Oswald, then call yourself into the ministry! Some preachers do! But there are people who think that we have too much man-strength now in our pulpits and not enough God-strength and that men who call themselves are not really needed. But you must examine your own heart and be your own judge.

I remember that Emma Alice has always wanted a preacher son. That is to be commended, provided you receive your call to preach from God and not from Emma Alice. Do not preach just to please your mother, Ozzy, for it will mean only one more inefficient and inadequate preacher thrust upon a long-suffering world. Also a good mechanic will be spoiled in the process.

In preparation for your work as a minister you will have had: 1) A very limited or no education; 2) a fair education; and 3) an extensive and intensive education. (Place an **X** after the one which best fits your case.)

There are many people and a few preachers who still believe that a preacher needs no education; that he needs only a Bible and that when he opens his mouth to speak

that God will fill it. Preachers of this type usually suffer
from spiritual malnutrition while their congregations have
been known to die of boredom and fatigue. If you have
(1) —see above classification—you can serve people of this
belief acceptably; also, you can boast of being a self-made
man.

If you have (2), you will find people everywhere to
serve; the world is long and very wide and is mainly made
up of people of this class.

If you have (3), you have only to disclose the fact and
churches will implore you to become their pastor.

But very serious difficulties arise when a number (1)
preacher takes over a number (3) audience. It is rather
like putting a number three shoe on a number seven foot;
in other words, a painful misfit. No, Oswald, if you are
a "Have-did" or an "I-seen" preacher, do not aspire to an
audience made up of intellectuals who read Greek for a
pastime. Some preachers do.

It is an advantage if you can write a great number of
letters after your name. It is best to be called "Dr." as it
gives you prestige. In the past it has been possible to
obtain this privilege for a modest sum from some junior
college. If it is not possible for you to do this, Oswald,
take a six weeks' course in chiropractic. A twofold value
will result. You may write "Dr." before your name, and
you can park one of those leather instruments of torture
in your parlor and earn an extra dollar or two, thereby
supplementing your income from preaching; and believe
me, Ozzy, you will need those extra dollars.

Whether you are entitled to it or not, insist on being
called "doctor." Fight for it if you have to; do not give in;
even your intermediates must not be allowed anything less
respectful. Keep it constantly before the people. This is
important. Never sign your name without your title and

degrees. As soon as you have your degree, write letters announcing the fact to all your friends. All of this will cause people to look up to you and to realize the important place you now hold in the world. It is important that you attend college at least one year so that you may refer in your sermons to "When I was in college."

You may need a good seminary to "salt" you down. So attend one if you can, Oswald. However, you may get more fun from fighting them than from attending them. Being a self-made man, you can prove the worth of your own attainments by denouncing all colleges and accusing them of "modernism" and heresy. It will be marvelous how many things you can find wrong with your denominational schools, and, of course, all state institutions are cesspools of iniquity operating chiefly to ensnare and ruin the youth of today!

You may prefer to work quietly and subtly. Openly you make reference to "Our Great Seminaries and Colleges" but to individuals you can speak your mind. In this way you can prevent gifts of money from going to these schools and perhaps keep a great number of young people from attending them. Also you will be able to enjoy that sense of importance that comes from being able to challenge and berate important individuals and institutions. Some preachers do!

Besides a regular "book education" you will need to know: 1) How to put up stoves and fit gas pipes; 2) how to pack china; 3) how to make a little money cover a multitude of bills; 4) how to make bookcases from a few odd boards; 5) how to refinish the top of a highly polished table after it has been moved, and when it resembles nothing so much as a roller-skating rink which has been constantly in use for many years without repairs of any kind; 6) how to make a sermon while the greatest bore relates his newest tale of woe; 7) how to operate a duplicator, a mimeograph, a saxophone and an outsize furnace; 8) how to make up to children and dogs; 9) how to wire a Christmas tree and set off tableau lights; 10) how to get rid of book agents (hint — perhaps the best way is to buy the book — speaking from our experience) ; 11) how to smile at a man when your natural impulse is to kick the seat of his pants; 12) how to eat anything and everything without asking the name, source, or previous condition of servitude; 13) how to remember every face you've seen once and every name called in your presence; 14) how to play football and tiddlywinks because of your young people; 15) how to sit on a keg of dynamite to keep someone from lighting the fuse. There may be others, Oswald, but these are a few rather important trifles that every minister should know.

Now that we have disposed of the matter of education, the thing to consider is the means of getting before the churches. Have a little book printed. Some preachers do. You will want a photograph made for it — one of you in a really striking pose; for instance, stand with one fist clenched and outstretched and hold your Bible uplifted in the other; stand on one toe with the other foot raised outward and backward as in running; wear a determined I-can-lick-the-devil expression. This pose is very effective. Wear a flower on your lapel or not, as desired. Another pose I would suggest is the melancholy, dreamy, intellectual one. Comb your hair back, disclosing a high, noble forehead; lean on your elbow, placing your hand at the side of your face in a graceful and artistic arrangement. Remember, Oswald, this photograph calls for Soul!

Place your picture first in the little book. On the page opposite the photograph have something like this, refined and elegant, but effective:

"Dr. Oswald B. Boloni, A.B., J.P., B.S. (Boy Scout), G.M. (Good Mixer), O.F. (Odd Fellow). Pastor, Evangelist, Trombonist, Philosopher, Author, Humorist, Crayon Artist, Poet, Musician, Exegete, Mathematician, Bicyclist, Seer, and Dyspeptic."

On the next page, something like this will bring results:

"Hear the Boy Preacher! This is your chance to secure this widely traveled, highly educated gentleman to be your pastor. He will draw big crowds; the house will be filled to overflowing after the first service!"

Send this booklet everywhere — to churches that are pastorless and to all your friends.

Another way to get before the churches, Oswald, is to use your friends and acquaintances. Of course, your few, real, close friends will be glad to recommend you, but do not stop with these. Write to friends of friends, and lay your case before them. Write something like this: "If you know of any up-and-coming church in good condition, paying about $3,000 per year, please recommend me for the place. If I do not get a bigger church soon, the ministry will lose a good man." Ask acquaintances to go with you to visit churches that are pastorless. It doesn't matter if they know but very little about you and your real qualifications — perhaps in that case they can recommend your services more heartily. Do not be afraid of embarrassing people; they have become accustomed to it through the years.

To get a really good church, a big one with a nice salary, apple-polish your state secretary or your presiding elder or bishop. Court the man — do favors for him, send him flowers on special occasions, flatter him, laugh at his jokes, slap him on the back. You might give this a good try. Some preachers do! If it doesn't work, you can always get even with him by telling everyone what a dictator he is (call him the Big Boss) — and what a dirty deal he gave you.

There are other ways that may suggest themselves to a fertile imagination; for instance, when supplying the pulpit for some brother pastor who is away on a vacation, or visiting his wife's mother, draw the chairman of the board aside and whisper something like this: "Are you satisfied with your present pastor? Do you think of making a change? If so, I would like to have the place and will be glad to take it for less money." The pastor, informed of this upon his return, will feel very kindly toward you, you may be sure, and no doubt the deacon will keep it in mind.

Offering to take a church for less money sometimes brings results; especially is the underbidding of men being considered by the pulpit committee very effective. Or make up to disgruntled church members and establish yourself in their good graces since they might call you after getting rid of their present pastor. Going on to a field and staying is one method I have heard of, Oswald, but do not try it unless you have plenty of intestinal fortitude. Some preachers do.

If you hear of a brother minister being ill, you might write to the church clerk something like this: "I hear your pastor is very ill. If he dies, I'd like to supply your pulpit with the view of accepting the pastorate." Enclose your picture and booklet. The man might die.

Or you might visit a number of your brother ministers and by means of adroit questioning ascertain whether they are considering a move or not. You can ask about the condition of the work, and whether they are satisfied or not, and what their plans are for the next year. Of course, they will never see through to your real motive and will only credit you with a kindly interest in their work.

It is one thing to believe in the leadership of the Holy Spirit and another thing to practice it. Many preachers interpret it as did the one who received an attractive call to a neighboring church. "Wife, you start packing while I pray about it," said he.

Perhaps as good rule as any to follow is this: Pray about it, do your best, and take what comes.

You will have some peculiar experiences with pulpit committees. They will ask you many questions such as, How is your wife's health, will she work with the women, how many children do you have (we do not want a preacher with a large family), and are you sound in wind and limb, are you considered a good mixer, how long did you stay in your last three pastorates, can your wife sing, are you a Republican or a Democrat, can you get out our bulletin, and are you good with young people? Put your best foot forward and let your light shine at these times. They may look up your past record, and check carefully on your work in other places. It might be a good thing to have always a record of honest, conscientious, careful, consecrated ministry behind you. This will help more than anything else in securing a place of service.

You will probably find yourself facing a situation of this kind: a small church made up of very contentious members who pay their pastor an extremely low salary, list their requirements for a new pastor. He and his wife must be well educated, both must be musical, he must be evangelistic; they must be good mixers and especially "good with young people"; they must be leaders in the town and be able to go anywhere socially. After hearing all of this, one prospective pastor announced, "If I were as good as you demand that I be, I would not be considering a church like this at *that* salary!"

You will not be called to various churches for various

reasons; they will think you too old or too young. They may consider you too fiery or too dull; they may not like your wife's "looks" or the way you comb your hair. One preacher was rejected because his wife did too much of the talking when the pulpit committee interviewed them. Another was passed by because his wife had the reputation of being a poor housekeeper. A church of our acquaintance always seeks a man "with a name, of whom we can be proud." This seems to be their only requirement. They seem to have forgotten that a church can "make" a man. They usually get their "man with a name" — and break him.

Some preachers have worked themselves into quite nice situations while holding services for brother pastors. One who is really clever can undermine the pastor and work himself into the good graces of the people easily enough. Just a hint here and there, an unspoken word, a glance, and a merry way with the ladies — and the pastor will soon be packing his books.

Last of all, Oswald, if all methods fail, you might try honest merit and prayer. In all this topsy-turvy world some still believe — and practice — and get results!

2

How to Keep It

Getting a church is one thing, Oswald, but keeping it is another. When your first burst of oratory is over and you settle down to a steady pace, will you wear well?

What is your plan for the church? Is it a one-year plan, a ten-year plan, or a twenty-year plan? Or, planless, do you mean to drift with every gust of wind, going backward or in circles? Or will you wander in a weak religious fog? Some preachers do!

From the very beginning, you will want to impress upon the folk that you have been places and have seen things. If you have been to Bermuda, casually refer to that trip in your sermons, taking many of your illustrations from your amazing experiences in that place. By skillfully interjecting Bermuda into your conversations and sermons, the impression will gradually get about that you are a man of the world.

Tell the people on the first Sunday that you are there, that when you have been with them six months you think that you can preach down to their level. The congregation will be sure to appreciate this.

Be superior. It will be well to let your people know that you know a thing or two. You must establish and maintain this attitude. This can be done by following these rules: Never see any side of a question but your own, or consider any opinions except your own. Resent suggestions from any source; for if you accept and act upon them it will practically be admitting the superior intelligence of others. Above all, be boss. Meet with every com-

Elbow the chairman aside and take charge

mittee — those on decoration, on painting the kitchen, on making Dorcas class yearbooks, on young people's picnics, on what to serve at the Mother-and-Daughter Banquet;

and at each meeting lay down the law; elbow the chairman aside and take charge; do not allow them to adjourn until you have had your way! This is important. If you are building a meetinghouse, by all means plan every detail and see that it is executed exactly as planned. Of course, if your ideas do not turn out to be practical or beautiful, you can always pass the blame along to the contractor or to the chairman of the building committee. When the matter of the kitchen is to be decided, it would be better for you to take care of that since the women never know their own minds. Plan the shelves, the arrangement of the tables, stoves, etc., and the size of everything, and do not allow the women to have any say about it; they talk too much, anyway. Tell them so. Some preachers do. But the main thing and important idea, Oswald, is to be boss.

It will be well, also, to let the members of your congregation know that you have been accustomed to better. A very fine way to do this is to introduce into sermons and conversations a rather wistful note as: "In Georgia we did not find it so." "The people are so different in Georgia." "When I was pastor in Georgia, we had a beautiful home." "The church in Georgia had an immense organ and a splendid organist." "They really sing in Georgia." "Our church in Georgia had the best business system I ever saw." "We had a lovely auditorium — so much bigger than this — in Georgia." "Our young people were so spiritual in Georgia." "They were very considerate of my wife in Georgia — she works too hard here." "The climate in Georgia is so much better." "You ought to see the peaches they grow in Georgia." "They have better roads in Georgia." And, Oswald, those who hear will never mind not reaching Heaven if they can only get to Georgia!

Express dissatisfaction often. Constantly keep before the

people the fact that you deserve something bigger and better. Tell them of offers you are receiving every week calling you to places where there are bigger and better churches that pay far greater salaries. All of this will make

Perhaps the threat would be safer

your people eager to keep you — or even give you a raise.

When things do not go to suit you, you might try the following (some preachers do): Resign or threaten to resign. Perhaps the threat would be safer. In spite of the fact that you would not mean them to interpret it literally, there is just a bare possibility that sometime they might take you at your word; and then, Oswald, where would you be? You would be that vest again hunting that pair of pants. So we advise you only to threaten.

Some preachers scold. Whether this will aid you or not in keeping a church once you have it is a moot question. You might try it. Every Sunday morning you can scold the absent members which will make the persons present feel guilty and uncomfortable even in the face of a clear conscience. You can scold the old people to the young people and the young people to the old people. You will have some telling results, I am sure.

If you want to keep your church a great many years, Oswald, mentally climb into a rocking chair and stay there. Some preachers do. Do not think deeply. Do not buy books. Do not read or study. Just let the Lord give you your sermons and it will be surprising how He will give you the same one over and over, until some unkind soul or critical being may actually suggest that you have only one sermon. Do not let it worry you. Of course, reading books written by other men is an admission that others have something for you to learn. Read nothing, and you can claim to be original.

You must make a fine appearance before your people, Oswald. Remember the old saying that clothes do not make a man but that they make 99 per cent of the woman; so your wife must have good clothes, too. You must live according to the very best and highest standards; your car must be new and of an expensive make — in short, you must have the very best of everything. If your salary does not permit this, charge these items. The church will not mind paying $500 or $600 after you are gone. Let your motto be, "The best at any price." The preacher who follows you on the field will enjoy paying your debts.

If you really desire to stay on a field a long, long time, having found your ideal parsonage, and church equip-

Then you will have a purged membership

ment, and town, just simply stay put. Let nothing short of a cyclone or an earthquake move you. Let hints roll off like water from a duck's back. If a committee talks it over with you, refuse to consider the remotest possibility of moving. People are alike everywhere. Why change one situation for another no better — perhaps worse? If you can hold out long enough your enemies will die or move away or decide it is too much trouble to dislodge you. Just stay. After all, what can the people who dislike you do about it except stay away from church?

If you do not want to move, do not find out too much about your congregation. It will eventually be brought to your attention that someone has stolen or misused funds, or has a social disease, or has rid herself of an unwanted child, or is having an illicit love affair. The people involved, when they know the pastor knows, will begin to work against him quietly, determinedly, until he is forced to move on to another field. He goes, wordlessly, not able to use the weapons put into his hand. Of course, Oswald, you *can* fight back — just try telling what you know and see what happens to you. A *few* preachers do! You can split a church this way and start a war in the town and get yourself sued for libel — some things are hard to prove!

Another way to keep your church is to clean up the membership roll. Begin with old scandals that you can unearth if you work diligently. These will be the basis for turning another group out of the church. You will then have a purged membership to work with, and should have no difficulty in accomplishing Great Things.

There are several other little ways to endear yourself to your flock. For instance, when a baby cries, shout, "Take that baby out!" If a girl has the nosebleed and is forced to leave hurriedly, stop preaching, stand perfectly still and glare at her until the awful silence condemns her as if she were willfully and criminally breaking up your service.

If things do not go to suit you, you can always get sore and quit. But remember, when you move you must take yourself along.

If, Oswald, you are a kangaroo preacher — always on the jump — here with summer, gone with winter, you may prefer staying only a year or two in a place. Some preachers do. In that case anything you do will not have much effect as you will soon be gone and forgotten.

3

Moving

Moving is either a form of torture invented by the devil to reduce a preacher to tears and madness, or a test permitted by God to teach him patience, endurance, and the control of tongue and temper. Let the harp represent the musician; the pen, the writer; the gavel, the judge; the skull and crossbones, the medic; the star, the detective; but, oh, my dear Oswald, for the preacher the moving van.

Whether you play that delightful little game "fruit basket upset," you know, Oswald, where everybody grabs a chair and the left one wails, or whether you belong to a more democratic organization that believes in each church picking its own, moving day — like the Day of Judgment — is inevitable.

You will either be called upon to move just when your garden is coming on, after days of back-breaking labor, and you will have to leave the tender young carrots, the thriving tomato plants, the tiny new peas; or you will draw a time when the thermometer is 8 below zero. If the former is true, you never move into the new place to find a nice garden left by your predecessor; you usually pay the trashman a dollar to haul away six barrels of junk left behind by the dear man. You survey the trash and think longingly of small new onions and little radishes left behind. If the latter is true — midwinter and beastly cold — you set your teeth and remember early Christians who were burned at the stake or fed to the lions.

The first step in moving is to systematically and thoroughly wreck the present living quarters. Put away in boxes all loose articles. There is no set rule for this. Your wife will always put the best glass and china in a box in the bottom of the van and the movers will place the piano upon it. Your most cherished picture will be discovered in a box with the ice tongs, the electric iron, and the portable typewriter, while Aunt Aurora's vase — which she gave you for a wedding present and you detest and fondly hope will be broken—is found packed in pillows.

You preach your last sermon where you are, and Monday arrives. You wreck the house. The trucks are scheduled to appear on Tuesday morning. The stoves are down and there is no food. You wait for the vans in anxiety and dirt. They do not appear. You buy a chunk of bologna, some crackers and doughnuts, which you eat wrapped in coats and rugs. (*You* wrapped in coats and rugs, not the bologna.)

Your wife says brightly, as she wipes Junior's nose, "The trucks will be here soon, I know. And won't it be lovely to see our nice, new home! I do hope someone asks us in to a good warm supper and to spend the night."

One o'clock, six o'clock; comes the dusk. You eat more bologna and a bakery pie for supper and unroll the mattresses and drop down on them still wrapped in coats and rugs and as many quilts and comforts as can be found not in use around clocks, lamp shades, mirrors, and vases. Comes the dawn. You eat more bologna and an orange. Oswald, Jr., says pathetically that he wishes he was at the South Pole; he couldn't be much colder and at least he'd have the penguins to play with.

Mrs. Long, good soul, brings you a pot of soup at noon

— which you, standing, eat out of glasses and teacups — and invites you over to her house for the afternoon and for the evening meal. You smile bravely and refuse; you might miss the trucks. You walk the floor and look down the street nervously; this, for four hours. For supper you have cold soup, hamburgers, and bananas. And so to bed. At midnight the family is peacefully sleeping when with a dreadful clatter and honking the vans arrive.

You work feverishly in the dirt and cold. By two o'clock you are going to your new home as tired, dirty and cold as it is possible for humans to be, but still game, still hopeful. You have forgotten the cat and little Oswald's red wagon and the lawnmower, but you optimistically look forward to other cats, other wagons, and other lawnmowers in the new home, so you say grandly, "Let it go." You will have forgotten to turn off the water, thereby furnishing scandalized comment for the deacons' meetings for months to come; and the wife forgot to turn the light out in the bathroom. Otherwise everything has been done and you go as blithely down the road as an undertaker walking down the aisle acting as an honorary pallbearer at a funeral put on by his rival in business.

As you ride, your wife says her head feels as if one of her headaches was coming on; that she hopes all this will not make Junior sick. She remembers that Junior was exposed to mumps some days ago and counts back trying to fix his time if "they" should "take" and decides he might have them any time now. She believes she has a fever. She hopes all this cold and hard work will not start up your neuritis again. She recalls that she has two teeth to be filled and that Junior's tonsils must be taken out. She hopes there are good doctors in the new town.

Junior says sleepily that his jaws hurt—"funny and awful bad." Mrs. Oswald says gloomily, "I told you so."

By this time you have arrived in the town where is located your new home. It will be almost morning, your wife will have a tearing headache and Junior will have been sick twice — what with the excitement, the cold and

Oswald, Jr. will have the mumps

the bologna and the bananas. Because you are rather low in funds (preachers usually are) you decide to stop at a second- or third-class boardinghouse, sleep a few hours, get warm, eat a hot breakfast and be on hand to help unload the furniture in the new home.

After much knocking, ringing, and waiting, you finally gain admittance, somewhat grudgingly given on the part of the host — even though the sign plainly says "Rooms for Tourists." The rooms are far worse than you expected, but you assure yourself that it is "only for a few hours," and so to bed.

You oversleep, of course, and after a hasty breakfast of pale and unpalatable food, washed down with quantities of bitter, thick fluid masquerading under the name of coffee, you hopefully drive to the parsonage. Be assured of either of two things. It will be very large or very small. If your former house has been tiny, the new house will be vast; if you have lived in a big house you will have the excruciating pleasure of adjusting your furniture to four small rooms.

After your first startled and bitter realization that you will have to get rid of half your furniture or buy that much more, depending on the house, you are aware of a line of children, round-eyed and staring, ready to burst into questions like pine shavings into flame when a match is applied. These are the neighbor's children. One will have a dirty nose and one will be broken out with a rash. You hurry Junior in, hoping desperately for the best.

There is an unwonted activity and bustle in the church next door. It tears into your consciousness that eyes are following your every move. You learn later that the ladies decided to give the church a thorough cleaning on that day — a coincidence, of course.

One comes forward to tell you (while the others listen) that the van has already come and unloaded, that everything has been put into the house; and that the men dropped one box and something broke; the ladies heard the crash distinctly; and that you cannot get the bed springs up the narrow stairs but that they will have to be hoisted up to and in through the window. Lucky it isn't the piano that must go upstairs!

You open the door and walk in. And, Oswald, my boy, strong men have been known to weep at the sight! (*Soft music here, and beat the drum slowly.*)

True, the furniture is all unloaded and in — in confusion, and presents an intricate jigsaw puzzle, requiring the greatest measure of patience, research, lifting power and endurance to solve. They have put the piano, Oswald, in the kitchen. The cookstove is in the parlor; the stovepipe has been carefully laid in the bathtub; and your books are all upstairs and the study is downstairs; the dining table is on the back porch and the garbage pail is in the front hall. You never find the ironing board or the top dresser drawer of your best dresser; and when you check up, your two best big pillows are missing.

If you have a stove, a new stove, Oswald, with six installments still due, the parsonage will have a furnace. If you have no stove and have had a furnace, the new house will have no furnace and you will be forced to buy a stove, a dollar down — easy payments.

Your rugs will be too big or too small. It is recorded that one preacher died of heart failure when he found that the kitchen linoleum from the old kitchen exactly fit the new. But do not worry, Oswald, this is an unusual case and will probably not come within your experience. The curtains, too, will not fit the windows. They are always too short, which will mean new curtains all around.

No kind soul comes to ask you in for a good warm supper and a good bed. You finally get a fire going and a bed up and creep into it, bruised and weary in body and spirit.

A PRAYER ON MOVING

(For Preachers' Wives)

Dear God, I do not know about Eternity—
Just where it is or how will Heaven be,
But this I pray—of wood or cloud or stone—
Oh, let me have a little corner for my own!
I've moved into so many houses in these years,
Have scrubbed so many boards and chandeliers,
So many sinks and pantries, tubs and kitchen doors,
So many halls and porches, walls and kitchen floors;
And when each room was home and clean and sweet,
The process in some other house I must repeat.
I've lengthened curtains; made them shorter by the hour;
I've planted seeds and could not watch them flower;
I've planned a room with rugs and drapes to be a lovely blue,
Then had to move it all into a room of scarlet hue.

Dear God, I do not know about Eternity—
Just how it looks or how will Heaven be,
But may I have a corner for my own, I pray,
And, please, may I not move—oh, let me stay!

4

Before and After

You will find, Oswald, that the Golden Rule applies to ministers as well as to the rank and file of humanity. It is a sound principle upon which to base your treatment of your fellow preachers as well as your fellow men. But you will find that in the ministry it is often sadly neglected or forgotten. Men who are otherwise conscientious and scrupulous seem to have no compunction in their dealings with their predecessors and their successors in the work; otherwise rational, they will develop "quirks" of jealousy and presumption that would not be countenanced in any other profession, and that seem unbelievable to the humble layman who expects the minister to be Christlike in all his dealings.

When the former pastor comes to town on a friendly little visit to people with whom he worked for years and whom he loves dearly, and comes in a spirit of good will and helpfulness to reinforce you and strengthen you all he can, sulk, Oswald, and ignore him. Some preachers do. Since you do not "run after" anyone, it will be best to avoid him carefully. If he is in the service on Sunday, do not ask him to preach or to sing; do not invite him to your home. Of course you are not jealous; you just feel he has enough to do at home without running into your territory.

If meeting and speaking with him is unavoidable, ask him if he writes to any of the people in that town; tell him that when you leave a place you quit it "cold" and that you never visit or have any communication with the people from that time on. Don't veil your sarcasm. Leave nothing to his imagination.

Tell him, in a brotherly way, of all the criticisms you have gathered up here and there, important and trivial, cutting or ridiculous, just or unjust, and firmly and kindly point out the mistakes he made, showing him how by your foresight and perspicacity you are managing far better.

A few good souls in your congregation and sundry of the townspeople will speak of the former pastor with good will and affection. You can meet this by answering with disparaging remarks concerning his character and attainments. Be quick to resent any compliment paid to the man or his work. Discount and belittle his record and accomplishments. Spread anything you hear to his discredit. Some preachers do.

But, Oswald, my boy, when the man follows YOU, it is so very different!

When you are leaving a church and your successor has been named, it will be well to see him in the beginning, or write him a letter, to tell him of the gigantic task found by you on the field when you first came, and of the heroic effort required to complete said task; of your high standing in the community; of your great success and popularity; of great favors shown you in every quarter; of your special training and fitness for that particular field, and that he cannot hope to "follow" you or attain to any measure of your standing and workmanship, or of the great esteem in which you are held by all the town. This will give the man the proper perspective of you and your work and will make him realize with humility that he is following a Very Important Man.

Go back to your old charge often. Run in — oh, every month or two; you know — pop in and out, for are they not your good friends? Why should you give them over to a stranger, a stranger of whom you think very little, anyway? If he should stay ten years on the field, you feel sure that the people will never love him as they love you. If he doesn't like it, he can just try doing something about it and break his neck—you would enjoy the process and rather hope to see it come to pass.

You still have the pastorly feeling toward the people, so encourage them to bring their troubles to you. Then go to the new pastor and tell him what they told you and what you told them and what his attitude should be. Give him plenty of advice as to people and methods, for you certainly know the field better than he does, and he should appreciate a little help from One Who Knows.

It is astonishing how many preachers there are who will ask with avid interest concerning their successors: "How is Brown getting on? Is he getting anywhere? Does he get on with old brother What-a-Grump? Are they paid up with him?" with a manner indicating that they expect to hear the very worst and to derive a certain relish from it. And pry, Oswald, pry. Run about collecting any information you can get (and there will be sources!) concerning your successor's methods of work, his preaching ability, his mixing, his financial plans, his doctrines (scent heresy if you can, and cry out in horror!), his family affairs, and his personal habits. You can keep things going so that the man will never know a dull moment.

Point out his mistakes to his people and whisper to them what you would have done under the same circumstances. Give your successor some more advice. Go back for funerals whether you are invited or not, and help with the arrangements. Since you know everybody so well your suggestions will be very welcome. Also solicit weddings. When an engagement is announced, appeal to the young people in this fashion: "Alice, I baptized you. Remember your promise, that I should marry you!" or "Gus, don't forget I married your father and mother. I expect to get this wedding. Drive over to Spring City when you get ready to be married."

Solicit meetings, too. Although the pastor may have another man in mind, and have his plans made, get two or three of your closest friends to present your name at the business meeting as the man they wish to hold the next revival. The pastor, being a fine, consecrated man, will not mind, but will cheerfully and gladly set aside his plans and will welcome you although he did not have a word to say about the whole arrangement, which was made secretly and which comes to him now as a great surprise.

When you hear of the growth of the church, the increased numbers, the great crowds of young people attending, the spiritual fervor, the sacrificial giving (although three or four years have elapsed since your leaving the community), be sure to take full credit for everything.

If possible, after you have resigned, live on the field. Then you can keep an eye on every little thing. You can be a wonderful help to the new pastor — calling on all the sick people, and on all of those not sick; giving him advice and criticism; helping him with plans and programs. You can quietly hold the loyalty of the people this way, too, and keep the man from becoming too popular and well established in his work.

5

Making Calls

Calling is at once the bane and the blessing of the minister's life. In rain, in sleet, in heat, in mud, in darkness, when sick or well, glad or somber, the minister must make calls. With the physician the minister stands by the sickbed and, with the undertaker, by the deathbed. He must visit the widow, the orphan, the discouraged, the spiritually hungry, the troublemaker, the complainer, the seeker, the doubter, the domestic fighters, the hysterical, the frivolous, the hypocritical, the scoffer and the proud. All of these he must meet and deal with besides making those friendly social calls among his congregation, expected by the people and enjoyed by the pastor as a normal part of his work.

A pastor may go night and day, work conscientiously and well, and be instant in his response to the call of distress or sickness or despair; and yet there will be those complaining, dolorous individuals in every church who will proclaim, "We like our pastor well enough, he is a good preacher, but he doesn't call." And, Oswald, have you noticed that the complainers are *always women?* I am old and full of years, but never yet, my boy, have I heard a man complaining because his pastor did not call. Why should any woman expect a busy pastor, who needs his time for meditation and study, to call on her when there is no particular need for his services, merely to chat for a few minutes on inconsequential subjects, listen to trivial gossip, hear a deal of "yammering," some confidential disclosures, and a great amount of slush? Yet, expected this sort of calling is, and it is one of the greatest bores of a pastor's life.

There are calls that edify, where one may give and receive help; but heaven help you, Oswald, when you start on your round of duty calls, merely to stop the critical mouths of two or three dozen cantankerous females with poor judgment and warped dispositions.

You will hear this criticism, too, Oswald: "I was sick and the preacher didn't come to see me." You will find out later that she only had a tooth pulled and that her next-door neighbor didn't even know about it. But she expected you to know all about it and to call.

Your membership will demand that you call. They will insist. Then, when you do, they will meet you at the door with, "You couldn't have come at a worse time! This is my washday — or I'm cleaning house. I looked for you all last week, and dressed up every afternoon and you didn't come." You apologetically make conversation for fifteen minutes and take your leave feeling as if you'd committed a crime.

Some people will expect and demand that your wife call with you regardless of the fact that Oswald, Jr. has the measles, and that the plaster has fallen in the kitchen, and that she has sprained an ankle. The show must go on! Others would rather you left her at home, anyway, since they (I speak now of the ladies) can become more arch and kittenish, and confidential, without the wife to spoil it all by her sensible presence. They will become lachrymose and frail and appealing, and will tell you that they are misunderstood by their husbands. So, Oswald, my advice is: Take the wife along and save yourself embarrassment. Get a neighbor to stay with Oswald, Jr., and clean up the plaster yourself; even carry your wife to and from the car, if the ankle will not permit her walking. But TAKE HER WITH YOU. It is better to feel overworked and downtrodden than foolish. You will soon learn from experience.

There are women in your congregation who will hate you if you do not "sister" them. Let them hate. It is better to have their ill will than to be involved in a scandal and lose your good name.

Of course, Oswald, you may be one of that brotherhood of granny-preachers who delight in being confidential with the ladies. In that case, leave the wife at home. Then you can have some of those intimate little chats wherein you confess that the wife never really understood you, and that you are simply perishing for want of understanding and sympathy. You can shed a few tears, gently hold the lady's hand at parting and feel you have at last found a true friend.

If these sentimental ladies are ill, you can have a grand time talking of illness, symptoms, etc., and giving good advice, being a sort of physician yourself, as it were. There are ministers who do not care for this sort of thing — but some preachers do!

When you call, you may wear your rubbers and carry an umbrella, or not, as you choose; or carry your gloves in your left hand or your right hand, and wear a flower or not, according to the degree of sentiment; there is no set rule. Emily Post does not cover this situation, and I have nothing to offer. But be prepared to discuss anything from kittens to curtains, herrings to harness, and second marriages to what-do-angels-wear.

Since nearly every home has its pet cat or dog, learn to

placate the animals by patting them with a nicety of manner calculated to allay any suspicion or irritation but not to encourage any undue familiarity. Otherwise, you may return from an afternoon's calling covered with cat

Make up to the children

hair or dog hair or with sundry snips taken from ankles, hose and trousers.

Always make up to the children. Take them on your

lap, dirty noses and all; but take it from one who is wise, Ozzy, right here *be careful*. Dire things have befallen noble men.

Make calls at all hours, in the night and at mealtimes — some preachers do. It is so uplifting to see the preacher walk up to the door when you have only hash and beans and bread pudding, and hardly enough of that to go around, and you know that it is his charming custom to just "drop in and eat whatever you have, like one of the family." Some preachers do.

Run to the hospitals at unusual hours. Burst into the rooms just when the patient has dropped off to sleep after hours of pain, or when the nurses are giving an enema to an already embarrassed and irritated patient.

Push past a "No Visitors" sign. Stay an hour. Give advice freely. Fidget and especially contrive to bump the bed. Discuss the election. Also an operation that you witnessed, just like the one performed upon the patient. Give all the horrible details and end with the pleasant information that the unfortunate victim died.

When they report the patient to be worse the next day, send flowers. Nurses are cranks, anyhow, Oswald, so if they hint that the patient must not see you next time, just go in, anyway, for a preacher could not possibly worry a patient. Everyone knows that a minister has special privileges. You can take advantage of the kindly attitude on the part of the public toward the clergy and do many things that other people are not allowed to do, Oswald. Some preachers do.

6

Weddings — Funerals — Baptisms

WEDDINGS

There are weddings and weddings. There are weddings at five o'clock in the morning and weddings at eleven o'clock at night. There are weddings in the pastor's home, in the bride's home, in the church building, in a friend's garden, in a boat and in an airplane. People are married in overalls, in print dresses, in satin and orange blossoms, in tuxedos, in white flannels, with coats or without coats; with ring and flowers, without ring and flowers, and sometimes with the proverbial shotgun. They come on foot, on horseback, in taxis, in ancient and complaining Fords, on motorcycles, and in the latest, slickest and most expensive cars.

The pastor's home is expected to be open at all hours to any wedding party. It is rather disconcerting at times — say, on a Saturday at noon, and the children dirty, with liver and onions cooking for lunch and the odor penetrating through the whole house, and the entire place in the throes of Saturday's baking and cleaning — to have a couple arrive to get married without any previous announcement. How hastily does the harassed Mrs. Oswald shut the onion smell into the kitchen, shoo the children into the back yard, slip a clean dress over her head with one hand, and with the other do a sleight-of-hand with the mop and other obscene housecleaning materials, all the while making a mental note that this job should be worth a five!

Whatever chaos may exist in the back part of the house, the living room always must be swept and garnished for "we might have a wedding." There is no discrimination as to the day; they arrive on washdays as well as on Saturdays or Fridays. They come when one is beating up an angel-food cake, or ironing the best linen tablecloth, or when one is taking a bath, or canning ten gallons of blackberries. All at once they are there. So there is nothing to do but put on a smile, pull up one's socks, and beam with delight. Sometimes one does get a five!

Anything, Oswald, may happen at a church wedding; so be prepared for any contretemps. You, yourself, may be the tragic victim of circumstances. One preacher, to my certain knowledge, went to a sunrise wedding, at five o'clock on a Sunday morning, wearing instead of a collar button a Boy Scout thingamajig to hold his collar to his shirt. In the dim light of early morning his collar button rolled away to parts unknown and in sheer desperation the clergyman borrowed the above-mentioned thingamajig from his small son. The ceremony was performed with none the wiser, except the preacher's wife, who was unaccountably nervous all through the service.

Now, Oswald, I want to give you the real dope on church weddings.

Like home weddings, they may occur at any hour, day or night. The type of clothes worn is indeterminate. The wedding party may be in street clothes or in sports clothes or in the most correct formal attire. The bride may wear any kind of dress or hat or veil and carry any sort of flowers, from gardenias to sunflowers.

Sometimes the groom forgets the ring or the license, or the bride is late. The pianist will make a false start or two, or the soloist will achieve a gurgle instead of a true soaring note. The soloist will sing anything from "O Promise Me" to "God Will Take Care of You." Two of the candles go out. These minor matters are forgotten as soon as the bride begins her long, slow glide to the altar. The groom slips out of the side door like a scared rabbit coming out of a thicket, preparing to make a dash for freedom. Only he never does. There are those in the audience who speculate on what would happen should he attempt it and hope some time to see it. The best man stumbles. The groom is in a trance. The bride fondly hopes that she looks like the latest newspaper glamour girl. The bride's mother is wondering if the ice cream will hold out and if Bridget will remember to thin the salad dressing, and if they made enough salad. The bride's father is conscious of next month's bills. Another splurge like this would put him in the poorhouse; he's very sure of that.

The minister looks the very acme of dignity. However, he is not musing on dignified nor heavenly subjects. Far from it; his mind is occupied wholly with an uncomfortable feeling in his stomach and he wonders if coffee could be causing his indigestion and notes that his coat is getting too tight. He feels sure that if he should stoop the thing would split. He resolves to breathe gently just to be safe, and immediately struggles with a desire to sneeze.

To go back to the bride: She advances down the aisle looking like an angel in her flowing white gown. The audience gently exhales in admiration. The groom slowly comes to meet the bride. Her lips move. The spectators suppose her to be counting, one — two — one — two — one — two —. What she really says is, "He's out of step!" referring, of course, to the groom. He, poor soul, comes forward on leaded feet. His thoughts are so muddled that they resemble a composite picture of the illustrations of *Alice in Wonderland*. His most coherent thought is strangely of the old swimming hole back of the pasture, out on the farm, and he decides he'd rather be there in its cool depths than anywhere else in the world; he notes idly that the preacher has an inordinately big nose; then realizes in desperation that the tall thing in white coming to meet him so inescapably is no one he ever saw before. She seems not to possess a familiar feature. How terrible; there is some mistake; he is resigned to marrying a complete stranger. Perhaps it *is* Sue, after all; but they have done things to her hair, and to her face with powder and paint.

They gather at the front. The ring is dropped. The replies are inaudible. The bride is a vision of loveliness and dainty girlhood. She seems to be a celestial being, fit only for heavenly places as she turns and floats down the aisle on the arm of her husband. As she nears the door, she opens her lovely mouth to speak. "This corn is killing me!"

And the food at weddings! There are proper repasts of correctly served dainties; and there are refreshments, especially at home weddings, calculated to throw one into mental spasms just from the effort involved in trying to figure out why soda pop and bananas are considered appropriate, and by whom; or why cheese and chili, or ham sausage and dill pickles, or why salmon mayonnaise at six o'clock in the morning.

They will always ask the minister, "Now what do I owe you?" and will pay you anything from a cord of wood to $25. Often you will receive a dollar from which you must deduct the cost of the certificate with which you present them, leaving you the nice sum of sixty-five cents for your trouble. They will ask you to drive them twelve miles in your own car, and promise to "see you Monday" and then forget all about it when Monday comes.

Yes, this business of weddings holds about it the thrill of the unexpected. So, Oswald, get yourself a nice long-tailed coat, and memorize a ceremony or two (which you will never be able to remember but must always cling desperately to your little black book) and put your living room in order and await weddings. Sometimes they come slowly, but sooner or later they come! And each one will be different and interesting, and a rich study in human nature.

FUNERALS

The hardest task the preacher has to face is the preaching of funerals, especially those of suicides or non-Christians. Many kind and lovely things may be said of the Christians at death. There is all the comfort of God to be offered to the sorrowing relatives of these. But how very difficult to find any message at all upon other occasions! And it is very strange, but often true, that the meaner the man, the more horrible his death, the more his relatives want a big church funeral. It may be that they feel that an ostentatious funeral in some measure makes up for, or disguises, the facts in the case.

A man may curse the church, and the preacher, and God, and yet when he dies his family will send for the minister and arrange for a church funeral. The man has never attended church, his family never go, they have never given a cent to the upkeep of the church, and now they never consider that it takes a ton of coal to heat the building; that men must obtain leave from their jobs to sing; and that the preacher stays awake all night wondering what to say. It does not seem to occur to them that they owe anything at all to the church or to the pastor for this service.

There are two lines a preacher may follow in preaching these difficult funerals. One is to preach all of them into heaven; the other is to tell the bald and unadorned truth. If you take either way, you are sure to incur the ill will of some of your hearers. You might try something like this: "He had no use for the church, for Christian people, or for God. He died as he lived and is at this moment burning in hell!" You may get by without being thrashed. Some preachers do.

You will doubtless receive many good suggestions from interested friends of departed ones. For instance, if Sam Endall blows out his brains with a gun, a good friend of his wife will tell you that Sam was a good man; that he was better than most Christians, and that she is afraid you will not do him justice. She will suggest text, sermon, songs and procedure, and will want for the poor sinful Sam's remains the grandest Christian burial!

Some preachers preach an hour and a half and preach hell-fire and damnation. Others briefly and hurriedly rush through the service, all the while fidgeting with the flowers, running here and there, getting in the under-taker's way, until the audience gets the jitters. You can do as you think best, Oswald. I know you believe in originality and freedom.

If you find it difficult to get a thought for a funeral sermon you might go to a member of the family and suggest that since you were not so well acquainted with the person that you might not say all the things they would expect, and please, couldn't this member of the family write a nice sermon which you would be very glad to deliver.

Of course there are books and things. You can quote

quite a lot of poetry and take up a great deal of time. See any good library.

And, Oswald, one other thing; you might refuse to preach any funerals unless well paid. This will make you popular in your community. Some preachers do!

BAPTISMS

A baptismal service may and should be sacred and holy and beautiful, but it also may be very grotesque. As in the matter of weddings, be prepared, Oswald, for anything.

There are large and weak-hearted ladies who may faint at the crucial moment. Go on and baptize them; water will bring them back. There are those excitable souls who are prone to lose their heads and whoop, "Boy, that water's cold," or some similar comment.

There is one little point to think about when you baptize in a baptistery. That is: what to do if and when your baptismal suit springs a leak. Several avenues of action are open to you. You can announce candidly that your suit has sprung a leak, that you are all wet, and that it is time to go home. If you baptize at the close of the sermon this would not be bad; but if, as many ministers do, you have the baptismal service first, it will be slightly embarrassing to send the crowd away. Very nonchalantly you might announce that you have decided to preach from the baptistery and that you believe in doing things your own way and not always following a set plan. Call for your notes and to bear out your alibi, have them sing a song with the last verse first and the first verse last. Not only will you conceal the fact that you are all wet but you will get credit for great originality. The only alternative left is to come forth boldly and preach, *wet,* which would no doubt be a novelty both to you and the congregation, who by this time will have learned to expect only dry sermons from you; they will be agreeably surprised for the once.

Some preachers keep the baptistery filled with water and ready for baptisms. I do not approve this method in your case, Ozzy, for I am afraid the baptistery would become a breeding place for mosquitoes and so endanger the health of your congregation.

You may decide to adopt the method used by certain denominations to save the bother of immersion. In that case, make a pretty little ceremony of it — dip a rose in water and gracefully flick the drops over the persons' heads. Allow them to keep their hats on. It has been done! Some preachers do!

7

Mannerisms

You will be told, Oswald, in schools and divers books, what *not* to do with your hands; but never will you hear or read anything about what to *do* with them. Doubtless with your deep intellect and ingenuity you can devise various ways to dispose of them while preaching.

There are preachers who wave them in the air and who pound the pulpit stand before them, rhythmically driving every point home. Pockets are a convenient parking place. A watch chain is a godsend since it can keep one hand occupied and will solve exactly one-half of your problem. The solution of the other half may rest with your glasses; they can be taken off and put on many times during a sermon. Yes, on the whole, Oswald, I believe the watch chain and the glasses to be happy solutions to the problem of what to do with your hands.

Some preachers have the delightful habit of clinking money, keys, or anything they happen to have in their pockets, while they talk. This is very distracting to the audience and will take the people's minds off the sermon. If you are conscious of having a very poor sermon, Oswald, try this little plan and your congregation will never discover that the sermon was not all it should have been. A disguise, so to speak, or a camouflage.

There are preachers who smack their lips and who mop

their brows in the course of their discussions. There are those who toy with a coat button, or with one ear lobe. There are those who repeat various phrases over and over, as: "More specifically," or "Enough of that," or "Listen

Pockets are a convenient parking place

to me," or "Dearly beloved," or "So far, so good." There are those who assume vulgar attitudes, disgusting and repulsive to people of taste and refinement, and who make

the audience body-conscious instead of sermon-conscious
— or Christ-conscious!

And, Oswald, please anchor your trousers firmly! After
one nerve-racking exhibition of unanchored trousers, one
poor soul left a certain church in a frenzy, mumbling
wildly to herself, "Oh, my Aunt Eliza! Thank goodness
they didn't slip." You can see, Oswald, that the sermon
was a complete loss to her.

It is surprising how many able and attractive ministers
there are who present an ungainly and awkward appearance when seated on the platform. They wind one leg
about the other like a bean vine around a pole; they
slouch; they sprawl; they sit with closed eyes; they look
heavenward with an assumption of piety; they thrust their
hands into their pockets and recline on their spines.

Remember, Ozzy, that any ridicule that falls upon you
will fall in a great measure upon the cause you represent.
Try to be dignified and courteous and well-bred at all
times; avoid giving offense to any person; and remember
that good taste demands certain standards of deportment.
It is possible that a church may reject a man because of
certain offensive peculiarities and mannerisms not accept-
able to people of good taste.

There are preachers who tear their hair and stamp the
floor; who thump the Bible; who jump into a chair and
out; who roar; who whirl like a dervish; who hop across
the floor with their arms waving, declaiming, "I am a
little bird, I fly, I fly!" In short, they act as if they were
fit for bedlam only and render an exceedingly attractive
gospel unattractive by their ridiculous and absurd mannerisms. It is enough to be a peripatetic preacher; pray do
not become a Punch-and-Judy one!

There are preachers who speak too slowly, with a pro-
longed "ah-h-h" at the end of words or sentences. Others

preach like a whirlwind, indulging in endurance and altitude flights, until their tongues become twisted and amusing statements result. Bear witness:

"He lives so far South that he can hear the roar of the

. . . an ungainly and awkward appearance

ocean waves when he sleeps in the daytime and when he walks about the streets at night."

8

Sermon and Program Planning

It is a very strange thing, Oswald, but people who can scarcely read or write their own names will be eager to tell you how to preach. They can tell you what, how, and when to preach, and hand out advice by the chunks. The less they know, the more they can tell you. The least successful man in your congregation will tell you loudest and oftenest how to succeed in your work.

You will find that numbers of high school and first-year college boys and girls will drop around to tell you how to run your church and what to preach. They will be very sure and earnest and strong in their convictions. From them you can find out what is wrong with you, your church and the world. Because they know so much, they will be your severest critics. If you want a lively time, Oswald, scrap with them; argue with them; call them flaming youth and preach on "The Wickedness of the Young People in Our Town." Some preachers do.

It is the average preacher's task, Oswald, to preach perhaps over one hundred sermons each year; men who are called on for addresses before colleges, clubs, conventions, etc., will perhaps find this number doubled. Then there are weekly prayer meeting talks, funeral addresses, and study courses, besides series of sermons for revivals. When the barrel is empty, what then, Oswald?

There are several ways to get material. For instance, there are excellent books on the market containing other men's sermons. Secure a good supply of these books, and memorize the sermons. Some of them may be recognized but then credit will be given you for having an excellent memory. Your hearers may think that Dr. Topmost got the sermon from you in the beginning; that he appropriated your sermon and put it in a book. This will gain you admiration and sympathy and cause indignation among your friends that the doctor could be so dishonest as to copy your original material.

When you run out of "soap," get some good stories and string them together. Tell a great number of other men's experiences as your own. Your congregation will never know whether these things happened to you or Dr. Truett or Dr. Boreham. You can get a vast amount of your material this way. Some preachers do.

Current events will supply a sermon or two. Fill in with jokes and wisecracks and much poetry. You can be indignant over any number of modern novels. This indignation can carry you through a Sunday evening or two. Special days will suggest themes, and all the year there are various holidays and seasons to work on, namely, Labor Day, Christmas, Halloween, first day of school, Thanksgiving, New Year's Day, St. Valentine's Day, ground-hog day, Washington's birthday, Lincoln's birthday, Fourth of July, All Fools' Day, the Ides of March, be-kind-to-animals week, fire-prevention week, safety week, good English week, eat-an-apple week, drink-sauer-kraut-juice week, Community Chest drive week.

Also nature will provide a subject or two. Drouth, earthquake, a Texas storm, a Kansas cyclone. There are expeditions and balloon flights to fill in with when these others I have mentioned are exhausted. You see, Oswald, in this little paragraph I have given you ideas for sermons for a whole year.

There are preachers who have worked out a very simple and effective system. They make one sermon and preach it on every occasion, just using one or two different stories each time and a new text, but always getting back to the same old sermon. People may well say of the preacher of this type, "He preaches a good sermon!" We read somewhere a story about apple pie that reminds us, Oswald, of some preachers' sermons. When asked what kinds of pie he had a waiter replied, "Two crust, one crust, and crisscross; but they're all apple underneath." You may not care to try this, preferring to use something more elaborate and intricate. But some preachers do.

It is necessary to give your sermons attractive titles if you expect to interest the people. You might use almost any little "catchy" phrase. It will not have to fit your sermon particularly, for as soon as you begin to preach your audience will forget what you called it. Here are a few suggestions that other preachers have used with success: "Poison Eggs and Spider Webs," "Sweet Sixteen, Never Been Kissed," "Little Red Riding Hood," "Autumn in the Ozarks," "Mules and Roasting Ears," "The Old Oaken Bucket," "The Devil and Tom Walker," "Baby's First Tooth." Others will suggest themselves to you, Oswald, like "All Policemen Have Big Feet," and "Where Is My Little Dog Gone?" and "Curfew Shall Not Ring Tonight." To make your list more complete you might add these: "There's a Reason," "Hell and High Water," "Bug Hunting," and "Hog Pen to Heaven."

You will want to make your sermons so unusual and interesting, Oswald, that they will stand out as something very unique and daring. I will suggest a few ways by which this may be accomplished. Preach in a soldier's uniform, boots and all, one night; another night, in regulation navy attire; again, don what the well-dressed golfer would wear and at a critical point in your sermon have a golf ball tossed to you by an accomplice in the gallery.

Make your sermons unusual and interesting

An interesting sermon topic is the story of David and Goliath, because in giving it you can demonstrate with a slingshot. You may throw your audience into an ecclesiastical dither which will not be held against you, since people will forgive you anything except their being bored, but do be careful not to let slip and smack a deacon in the eye, provided, of course, that you have a deacon present.

In planning the program of your services, Oswald, be very careful that everything is appropriate and harmonious. It is surprising the music that some organists and choir leaders consider suitable for church worship. I, with my own ears, have heard in a Sunday evening service, a young woman blandly play on a Hawaiian steel guitar, to the horror of the minister and the congregation, that little masterpiece, "One, Two, Three, Four!"

One pianist will conceive the idea that the "Kerry Barn Dance" is just the thing to play for an offertory. Another will launch into "Stars and Stripes Forever," and the sentimental soul will wistfully and softly wring from the keys the haunting melody, "Gypsy Love Song."

When in doubt as to a recessional, I would suggest "To the Regions Beyond I Must Go, I Must Go." Also this is very good for a funeral march, Oswald, as is "I Dreamed I Searched Heaven for You."

At a recent church service we couldn't understand a word the soprano soloist sang. The preacher's wife thought she said "Grace before meat." The preacher thought it was "Thy face do we greet." But I felt sure she was singing "This pace hurts my feet." If your soloist and choir members could only learn to speak distinctly it would help the services *a little*.

Your choir will prove to be a constant source of worry and trouble. The young people will not want to sing with the older people; the older people will resent the young ones; the latter, having been well-trained in school choirs, will probably read music with ease; the older ones

will complain that the music is too hard and too "hifa-
lutin" and will develop a touchiness because they read
music with difficulty. Some of your people will favor the
fine old dignified church music; others will like the banjo-
guitar school of tinkle-plunk. Between them all the pastor
has a most interesting time. You will even hear this, after
the choir has sung a number involving a soprano obbli-
gato, "I wish our choir could learn to sing together! In the
anthem this morning that soprano was two jumps ahead
of the choir all the way through!" And here your choir
director will meditate mournfully whether he should go
back to the farm, join the army, or end it all.

Talking of solos, Oswald, it will not matter how burning your sermon on repentance, salvation, the Cross, or
hell, your soloist probably will warble a little thing that
has to do with gardens and birds and brooks and trees
and flowers that bloom in the spring, tra-la. Church solo-
ists so often wish they were apple blossoms or extol the
beauty of sunrises, or sing of God and you and a star,
that long before they have finished the song the audience
is so weak and numb, what with trying to understand
the words and all, that they never revive enough to pay
any attention to the preacher or the sermon.

There may be in your audience, a sin-sick soul — one
perhaps on the verge of committing suicide, weary, dis-
illusioned, groping, in agony of spirit, who comes to the
house of the Lord to seek Him. Your reedy tenor or
filtered soprano singing of apple blossoms or gardens will
be of great help, I'm sure. His thought of committing suicide will only be hardened into decision under the spell
of these nice little songs.

We need more and better songs in our churches to show
forth, not babbling brooks, but the Living Water; not
apple blossoms, but the Lily of the Valley and the Rose of

Sharon; not little lambs at play, but the Lamb of God; not the birds that build their little nests, but the Shadow of His Wing; not beautiful little hills, but the City of Refuge; not trees, but One Tree — the Cross of Calvary.

Of course, Oswald, being Emma Alice's son, you may like the birds and the bees, the brooks and the trees. I remember that she always had a weakness for the little rhymes concerning daisies and birds and shy little violets beside a mossy stone. In case, Ozzy, that you prefer this type of music, and the proper little sermon-lectures that go with it, there are other churches to which people will go who really need help and guidance and food for the spirit. And do not think for a moment that they will not go there. They most certainly will.

In many of our churches, Oswald, logic and reason and intellect have put on long-tailed coats and occupy the pulpit, while repentance and faith and love — beggars all — twiddle their thumbs on the back seat. Art, in glittering and alluring robes, presents to all who enter a silver cup called beauty which, being quite empty of the Living Water, offers no alleviation of the crying thirst of the multitude.

Without doubt, Oswald, the multitude is thirsty and hungry for that which Christ has to offer. Will you send them away empty? Or will you earnestly strive to bring your audience to the throne of grace? Some preachers do!

The little poem that follows seems to express, at least to me, the responsibility of ministers to satisfy the longing of mankind for the strength and the help and the guidance that come to the person who puts his faith in the unmatchable Christ. The world is waiting to be told of His love and grace; and some preachers do preach that beautiful message.

A PLEA

You have builded temples in His name
  Of mortar and brick and stone,
With windows of glass most beautifully stained,
  With tower and spire and dome;
But what do we of the byways care
  For structure and line and trim?
Out in the dust of the lonely road
  We only ask for Him!

You have blazed His name across the night
  In letters of flickering fire;
In rainbow hues you have said, "Come in";
  You have shouted your desire;
Oh, what do we care for the many lights
  When our heart's high hope is dim?
Show us the light of Bethlehem's star
  That we may go to Him!

You have robed your choirs and trained them well
  In proper and intricate song;
You have bought fine organs to edify
  And lull the weary throng;
But what do we care for your black-robed choir
  Or your organ's deep Amen?
Unless you will walk beside us here,
  And point the way to Him!

What do we care for temples and spires,
  For pomp and riches and fame?
We cannot see them through falling tears—
  Who are sick and blind and lame;
You have pointed the way to temples tall;
  To your music grand and sweet;
To logic; to art; and to intellect;—
  But we seek the print of His feet!

The roads of the world are a crooked maze,
 And we are woefully lost,
For the road to Him in the paths of men
 Is faint and hidden and crossed.
Oh, what do we care for the trappings of Art
 When our heart's high hope is dim?
We seek the touch of His healing hand,
 Oh, show us the way to Him!

In planning your programs you will always find this true, that there are mothers and friends of would-be singers or readers or pianists, who will call you to ask that Jemima or Marcus be put on the program. "It is so good for the children to perform before the public, and she (or he) really has a lovely little piece (to play or sing or recite), and her (or his) teacher says that the child is positively marvelous."

How many doting mothers have thrust their frightened offspring upon a long-suffering congregation "for practice"!

You won't dare refuse, Oswald, for the mother will withdraw her support from the church and Grandma and Aunt Elsie will follow suit, and since you need all the financial aid and good will that you can get, you put Jemima's name down on your program for "I Know That I Shall Never See," or "Nearer, My God, to Thee" (with variations), or "Little Willie's Prayer," and endure silently!

Your prayer meeting will require very little thought and effort. Wait until ten minutes before the time to begin the meeting and then hurriedly select a few verses of Scripture, at random, and use them as a basis for a "few feeble remarks." Some preachers do! And wonder why the attendance at prayer meeting becomes smaller and smaller!

But however hard your work, whatever you do, no matter how well you plan, the meeting will probably resolve itself into the "usual" church program: "We met, set, and et."

Another God-wotter

9

Advertising and Revivals

If you want to be a modern, successful, up-to-date preacher, Oswald, it is absolutely necessary that you advertise! And why not? Banks advertise, and the picture industries spend millions advertising. Look what advertising has done for halitosis and B.O. And but for advertising, would you have known that Heinz has fifty-seven varieties? You would never think of over thirty-two or forty-nine. It pays to advertise!

The papers first present themselves to our thought. Bluff, bribe, or pester the editor of your paper into printing long articles, all written by yourself about your own comings and goings and doings. If you are appointed on a P.T.A. committee; if you go to the city to buy a new suit; if you have a paragraph printed in your religious paper, demand a front-page writeup; or still better, write the article yourself — you can really do greater justice to the subject — and insist that it be published in a prominent place.

Do not neglect your own denominational papers. Report once or twice weekly. Not a modest report of a modest growth — this will get you nowhere. Let people know that you are on the map and doing things. Report something like this: "We have the biggest Sunday school between Chicago and New Orleans. Great crowds at preaching services, standing room taken, many turned away! Greatest day in the history of this church. We have been here two months and the attendance at all services has doubled! Greatest singing I ever heard; greatest choir. Finest young people. Fine weather, wonderful people, splendid town. Pray for us."

The only prayer that will come to the minds of some of your readers, Oswald, will be one that you will accidentally hit a nail or a pin and burst. But these people will be the ones who are jealous of you, so do not worry, my boy; just go right on with a good strong letter each week.

People will never know your true worth unless you tell them, so advertise by word of mouth. Tell them that when you lived in Illinois you built an "$80,000.00 church building"; that you are a bosom friend of the great Dr. John Will Grow, and that your wife is a cousin of the famous Dr. Bluster.

Yes, Oswald, it pays to advertise. Do not neglect a lavish use of your photographs (the papers will be *so* glad to get them) and of trick cards calling attention to yourself and your high position. Work yourself into schools, clubs, anywhere to be seen and heard. You want people to know you just as they know Burma Shave and Mother's Oats. Advertise! Some preachers do.

Some little fellows, Oswald, would never be noticed at all if they did not make a noise. A sage has remarked that the "lost man hollers." And the deeper he gets into the woods, the louder he hollers. There are men who make up in noise that which they lack in ability — like little Jimmy in the back yard who yells ear-splittingly, "Look at me! Look at me! I can turn a handspring — look at me!"

When you are preaching in a revival meeting remember your advertising. Your next engagement may depend upon your glowing accounts of the present meeting. Great numbers of additions are most desirable and will put you over, so never neglect an opportunity to count hands and noses. You can easily persuade a number of small children to come forward so that you may report in the next issue of your denominational paper, "Thirty forward. Great day."

For your convenience, Oswald, it might be well for me to outline the order of service followed by some revivalists. Then you will have a foundation upon which to make your own plan.

First, you must get everybody into a happy frame of mind, which can best be done by having a snappy song service. Your song leader must have pep. He must call upon the people to sing. "Now si—i—ing, everybody. Unless you've had a quarrel with your wife, si—i—ing." He must tell a few good stories between songs. He must urge the people to "step on the gas" and push out the sides of the house, on such favorites as "Brighten the Corner" and "Hallelujah, Thine the Glory." When he sits down beaming and perspiring, you come forward and announce that you will take the offering. That if they want a whale for a preacher, they must supply the water for him to swim in. Call out each deacon by name and tell him to walk up and lay down a dollar; if he hasn't one, to borrow it, hallelujah. Get every cent you can. Then have a song. "Must I Go, and Empty-handed?" will do — and launch into a dramatic sermon on "The Circus of Life," in which you imitate the various animals, side-shows, and entertainers, or on "Hold That Ball," in which you enact a football game ending with a touching refer-ence to playing the game fairly and to the greatest player of all, Christ, and will not everyone there get into the game? Count every raised hand, sing the doxology and dismiss.

You can vary this program a little from night to night. A clever mind like yours will be able to think of many novelties and unexpected treats, I am sure.

And remember, Oswald, any man away from home is a big man, so when you are the visiting minister it is well to be fussy about beds, meals, and arrangements in general, so they will know that you are accustomed to comfort, ease, and elegance at home.

During a revival, you will find that as a visiting minister you will be royally entertained. The ladies will vie with each other in setting out rich and delicious foods. One way to be different, Oswald, is to look over the table wistfully and ask for a "small piece of dry toast and a little tea." Your hostess will perceptibly diminish and will weakly go kitchenward to prepare it. Then on your way home you can drop by a restaurant and get a big, juicy steak, bountifully surrounded by all the trimmings, for yourself.

Of course, you can announce publicly that you never eat cake, pie, or chicken, or in fact, meat of any kind — or rich salad — or hot breads. That people are not to go to any trouble for you. Some ill-mannered brute may ask if "the nut can suck a bottle," but never you mind, Oswald, never you mind.

You can't afford to underrate yourself, for others might take you at your own estimation. Therefore, place a high value on your services. When you are preaching for a series of meetings or for some special occasion, it will be best to appear dissatisfied with the amount tendered you in return for your labors.

You might prove your worth by holding up to ridicule both the town and the pastor, and by being abusive in your speech in the pulpit, which will get the pastor and the people into a properly humble frame of mind.

Very often, during the evangelistic campaigns, you will be housed in the home of the preacher. Whether this be true, or whether you stay with some good member, have all your laundry delivered to the home in your absence, which will necessitate your host paying for it. Also have him receive all C.O.D. packages. Let him pay your cleaning and telephone bills. Then depart without so much as a "thank you." One way to do this without embarrassment is to toss the unpaid bills into your hostess' lap with a laughing little remark, "I'll make you a present of this." Some preachers do!

Do not be surprised if at some time in your career you run into this one: You do your best preaching, day and night; the results are satisfactory to all concerned. Everyone seems pleased. A nice offering is taken for you. Then the pastor and the deacons decide to keep half of the money to pay the back bills of the church. In this case, nothing can be done, Oswald, except to quietly ooze out of the picture.

One of the hardest tasks of all is that of holding a revival meeting when the church and the pastor are at outs, and each approaches you with his side of the story, expecting to enlist your sympathy. Your meeting is doomed before it begins unless you are astute enough and godly enough to bring the disagreeing ones together for a fresh start. Of course, you can take sides and make things worse. Some preachers do!

Now, Ozzy, my boy, I am going to let you in on a nice little "racket." This is called the "Sympathy Line." Every night during your meetings, tell the good people about the great troubles that have come upon you; that your oldest daughter is threatened with tuberculosis; that your wife is

in wretched health; that you have a hospital bill of approx-
imately twelve hundred dollars to pay; that your Aunt
Minerva has lost her money and has come to live with
you; and that you have worked *so* hard this year, and that
your health is so very poor; and that you have lost your
savings in a bank failure (of course, this is purely for
effect, since you have never had a penny in the bank, but
have always owed money there!) and that you must
depend upon these fine Christian people for help. They
will pour out the money. Then some of the fine, Christian
people will decide that you need the money more than the
pastor needs it (who is given the princely salary of $12.50
per week) and will withdraw their support from him,
and send you their contribution each month. By working
this game carefully you can have a host of contributors
over several states insuring you a fairly good income. Some
preachers do!

10

The Preacher's Wife

For the sake of clearness and brevity, I will tell what I know about preachers' wives in two sections, Oswald. In one will be advice for Mrs. Oswald; in the other, advice for the congregation. I suggest that Emma Alice read the latter part for she has always been addicted to Rule Number Eighteen.

It would be well, Oswald, to announce on your first Sunday in a new place, that your wife is *your* wife; that she is not employed by the church and that you will not have her overworked; that she must not be asked to do anything, and that people must not expect her to make calls, teach, sing, or take part in the women's work, since she is not very strong. She may really be as hearty as an ox, but saying the latter will help you to put your point over.

Tell the women that your wife is just recovering from a very serious operation, but neglect to mention the fact that said operation took place two years ago; let them know that she really should not lift heavy furniture or get too fatigued. With great sympathy the kind women of the church will come in and do all the hard work for her. An operation is very useful at times.

It might be well to let them know that where you last lived someone always came in and took care of the children for a few hours each afternoon, giving your wife time for a good rest. Complain bitterly if this idea is not immediately carried out.

The I-have-seen-better-days attitude is sometimes used to an advantage by some preachers' wives. This consists of touching references to "when I was a child at home." "We had private teachers; we had an enormous house; we had colored servants; I was the only child and had everything I wanted; I had so many lovely clothes; we had our own stables. Our family is one of the fine old Southern families." The people of the church will begin properly to appreciate you and your sacrifice in giving up so much to serve them.

Then, too, you must be high-hat with people, Mrs. Oswald. Never allow them to undervalue you. And, above all, achieve and maintain a position as dictator of all the activities and policies of the women of your congregation. Be the final court of appeals and the supreme judge. Let them know that you know just how things should be done and that you mean to have your way. Some preachers' wives do.

If you are a musician, take over the piano or the organ at once. Do not allow anyone else to touch it. Sing all the solos and the solo parts yourself. It might be well to lead the choir. Be the assistant pastor. The pastor's wife in every church holds a unique position of trust and authority by virtue of her office; you can presume on this power that is yours, Mrs. Oswald, and use it in various ways to dominate and manipulate the affairs of the church. Some preachers' wives do!

Church work is so much more important than housework that you can pay scant attention to the latter. People must not expect too much of you. You can excuse yourself by telling people prettily that you are a Mary and not a Martha; that your church comes first in your life and that since your husband's salary is not sufficiently elastic to cover the expense of a maid, you just let the housework go. Some of the ladies may come in and help you clean occasionally. If people must run in at all hours, they can just expect to find the house all upset. You hate housekeeping, anyway!

A few cases are recorded of able and consecrated men who never stay on any field for any length of time because of sloppy and slatternly wives. These poor, bewildered ministers wonder why they always seem to be misfits when they try so hard to please and are sincere preachers of the Word. The real reason is the condition of the home and the attitude of the wife. More preachers have been ruined by misfit wives than have been ruined by sin and the devil. On the other hand, preachers have been made by women who stanchly and prayerfully and adequately carry on their tasks—encouraging, inspiring, leading, and praising. These wives realize that clean minds require clean and sweet surroundings, and so they do their part, making much of little in the house; seeing that the children are well fed and rosy and fresh and crisp, and that the ways of the household are well ordered; finding time somehow to do it all cheerfully and well. Some preachers' wives do!

Dress well; dress beyond your husband's means. Charge things. A certain standard of living must be maintained. He can't expect you to look a frump just because he is a preacher. If the people would support the church properly, you could pay your bills. Tell them so. Anyhow, if you can't pay the bills, the church can. Or let your husband figure out some way to pay them. You just have to have something decent to wear.

One way to be popular with your church, Mrs. Oswald, is to permit little Oswald, Jr. to whittle on the woodwork and many floors of the parsonage, and to draw crayon pictures on the walls. The Ladies' Aid will enjoy the little darling's efforts to express his artistic yearnings, I am sure.

The Ladies' Aid will enjoy artistic efforts

Let your own children run loose. While you attend church meetings they can stay with your neighbors, who will be glad to wipe their noses, tie their shoes, and give them bread and butter. Never see the faults of your own children, but criticize the manners and the conduct of the children of other people. Talk about them for doing the very things your children do. Resent any friendly little reproof given your child by some member of your congregation whose only motive in speaking is the child's well-being.

Do not forget that you are only a member of the church like anyone else. Stay at home just like other people when you feel so inclined. Do not attend prayer meeting or any other service unless you feel like going. Other members stay away — why not you? They should not expect any more from the preacher's wife than they do from other members of the congregation. You might even attend some other church of your denomination in your town (a bigger one than the one where your husband preaches), and, of course, one with a pastor who can preach better than he. In this manner you can escape some of the duties and obligations that will fall upon you in your husband's church. Some preachers' wives do. But really, Mrs. Oswald, this course of action will seem to mean that you are ashamed of your husband, and will be a great handicap to him. There are those, to be sure, who might think that it would be a greater handicap to have you present. But that is a moot question.

Some preachers' wives go in for society; you might try this — if you can break in. Cultivate the smart set in your town with the attitude that there are so many common people in your church and that you are so far above them. Your people will love this!

Be a helpful little wife. Criticize your husband's sermons and his manners. Do not wait to do this privately. Tell him before people so they will know that he wouldn't amount to a thing if you were not constantly at him.

Select a few of his little weaknesses and make fun of them slyly to other people. This is very effective.

Tell everyone that you married your husband, not because he was a preacher, but in spite of his being one. Or this one will do: "I didn't know he'd ever preach when I married him," with the inference that getting into the ministry is a sort of disgrace, like getting into jail — or politics. Or you can sing a little song like this: "I want to live on a farm."

Thus will your husband be successful and happy.

And, lastly, Mrs. Oswald, permit me to say that the time will come as inevitably as the watermelon season or washday, when someone will knock at the back door, the front doorbell will ring, the dinner will boil over, and the telephone will scream — all at once. You can either yell "No" at the back door, "Wait" at the front door, "Hello" at the telephone, turn the burner out under the dinner, or just kneel in prayer. Mrs. Oswald, you must rise to the occasion graciously, as befitting one not made of common clay. You may find a way to do it. Some preachers' wives do.

PART 2

HOW TO MAKE A PREACHER'S WIFE HAPPY
(For the Congregation)

RULES:

1. When the new minister and his wife arrive, before she removes her hat or unpacks the dishes, telephone her that she will be expected to teach a Sunday school class, become president of the Missionary Society, sponsor a young people's society, and teach a training class.

2. Call her to the telephone often; any trivial matter will do. See that the phone rings twenty or thirty times each day; it will keep her mind off the ironing, cooking, washing, etc.

3. Repeat loudly and often that she has not been in your home. Do not call on her yourself, but expect her to call on you within a week of her arrival in the new parsonage.

4. Expect her to make calls with her husband. Do not consider that she has the care of a family and a home, and must cook, clean, sew, and mend, just as you do — besides meet all the social obligations forced upon her as the minister's wife.

5. When she comes to see you, talk of nothing but the former pastor's wife; tell her how Mrs. Blank managed everything perfectly, and make her feel that she can never live up to Mrs. Blank. Upon every occasion say, "Mrs. Blank did it this way."

6. If the minister's wife sings or plays the piano, show jealousy. Criticize her for singing too often. If she plays, do the same. Tell the world that Miss Minor Key is a far better singer and pianist. If she does not sing or play, feel sorry for the minister because he married a "dumb-bell." Tell everyone she is not "fitted" to be a minister's wife.

7. Expect her to remember names and faces perfectly. Get peeved and stay away from the church if she doesn't know you the second time she sees you.

8. Give five cents a week to the church, and then howl because the preacher's wife wears the same old hat for four years.

9. If she is very friendly, tell everyone she gushes. If she is shy and reserved, say that she is proud and "stuck-up."

10. If she has small children, expect her to do a vast amount of church work. She can manage somehow.

11. Within her hearing, repeat often that preachers' children are always worse behaved than the children of other people.

12. If she is not well, say it is all "put on" — that she does not want to do church work.

13. Send your children over to spend five days a week. Get peeved if she sends them home. Send them over when she has company. Allow them to stay for meals. Permit them to look in all the closets and dresser drawers and cedar chests and cabinets.

14. Talk about all the church members; if possible, go over the first week and tell her all the scandal and gossip of the last fifty years, and do not leave out the up-to-date news.

15. Berate the former pastor and his wife.

16. Insist on her entertaining all visiting preachers and workers. Never do any of this yourself.

17. Insist on her coming to Ladies' Aid and quilting one day each week. There you can tell her so many helpful things — that it is extravagant to buy ready-made dresses; that her husband's sermons are too long or too short; that he should be a better mixer; that you do not like the way she fixes her hair. She will love the advice.

18. Invite her to all class meetings; put her on all programs and make her a member of all committees; insist that she train the children for all special programs, then *ask her what she does with her spare time.*

19. Make remarks about her new clothes. Tell her she has too many new dresses and you do not see how she does it on her husband's salary.

20. Use the parsonage for a public waiting and rest room. Have all music rehearsals there; never bother to

ask permission. Take your children over there to spank them and to change their diapers during church services. Run in without knocking until the pastor becomes nervous every time he changes his pants or is taking a bath.

21. Then buy her a nice white lily. By this time she will be perfectly happy, having entered into the joys of the Kingdom and attained her heavenly reward.

22. Obtain a beautiful stone. On it engrave: "She hath done what she could — and what she couldn't, killed her."

11

Conventions

A convention, Oswald, is a body of preachers entirely surrendered to gab. You must make it a point to attend conventions, otherwise you will be a back number, having missed all the oratory, the scheming, and the wire-pulling common to these meetings.

The most important thing for you to remember is that you must make yourself known, and must stand out from the common crowd. There are several ways to achieve this.

Some preachers try to be different by dressing in some striking manner to attract the attention of people. Surely you will wear your professional coat. Perhaps you can assume a distinguished look by allowing your hair to grow long and wearing it slightly rumpled à la Paderewski. Try wearing odd- or unusual-shaped eyeglasses, those with a long cord — you know, as if you had your eyes on a leash and were leading them about. A ten-gallon hat is very striking for convention wear.

Keep busy at something. Hand out programs and song-books. This will necessitate much running about, up and down through the aisles; it will give the effect that you are one of the big men of the convention and responsible for its well-being and progress.

Be seen with the more important men. Cultivate their friendship. Be persistent at all times. This is important. Then you can say, "Jones said to me," referring to the

president of High Voltage University, or "my dear friend
George [Dr. George Moore Piety] told me this story."

Slap the other delegates on the back familiarly when you
meet them. Nudge them during the speeches, to show

Lean for support when laughing heartily

them that you got the speaker's point, and wish to call
their attention to it. Lean on them for support when
laughing heartily at the jokes from the platform. People

who see you in such company and on such free and easy
terms with them will assume that you are one of the choice
group. This will be very gratifying to you.

In order to be known to everyone in the convention,
rise to your feet when opportunity offers, to take part
in the discussions. Make your talk snappy and vigorous,
impressing upon your audience your easy flow of words
and your perfect poise and good judgment. Talk as often
as the chairman will allow. If he calls you down, do not
be discouraged. Rome was not built in a day. Some men
are too jealous to recognize a man of wit and brains; they
will want to keep you in the background, but you show
them. Remember, the best apple tree in the orchard
always has the most sticks thrown at it!

If you are given a small part on the program, do not
consider it as small. Regard your part to be as important
as that of the main speaker on the program. Be brilliant
and witty, and your audience will be delighted to stay and
listen to you an hour or two beyond the expected and
normal closing time. You will wonder why you are left
off the program next time. Some preachers do.

Another way to achieve prominence and to gain the
limelight, is to show up the little fellows. Pick some self-
educated man who is earnestly defending his side of
the question. Make a speech opposing his views and
close with a scathing denunciation of your opponent —
"Brethren, this man never saw the inside of a seminary!"
This will cause you to be admired as a plain, outspoken
man, fearless in his speech. Some men may want to punch
your head, but remember, Oswald, it is just envy — just
envy.

In order to keep your name before the convention, it
might be well to arrange with your wife and a few close
friends to have you called out to answer the telephone or

to receive telegrams frequently during the convention sessions. It sounds well to hear your name called at a banquet — "Dr. Oswald Buggs Boloni wanted at the telephone." "Dr. Oswald Buggs Boloni, a telegram." People will whisper, "He must be very important and much sought after. He is a Big Man."

Everybody takes notes at conventions. You will want to follow the usual custom, so secure a small notebook and a dull and inadequate pencil. Personally, I am always reminded of Bill the Lizard (in *Alice in Wonderland*), when I am in conventions and watch people take notes. The notes they take are about as important and coherent — and last about as long — as those Bill took on his slate with his finger. When some impassioned speaker rises on his toes and shouts, "Ours is a stupendous task," write "Ours is a stupendous task." When he cries, "These are perilous times," write earnestly "These are perilous times." When he begs for a deeper prayer life, write "More prayer."

Two weeks later when you look these notes over, they will resemble a recipe for Hungarian goulash, written in Hungarian, or a Chinese laundry ticket. Your notes failing you, when you report the convention at home, you can say what all the delegates will say who find themselves in similar circumstances — "It was a most wonderful and inspiring convention. The address was just wonderful. I wish you all could have been there. I received great inspiration."

If the entertaining church is providing beds for the visitors, go to a hotel without consulting the committee to see if hotel rooms are included in the arrangements. Check out without paying the bill, and tell the clerk to collect it from the church as they were supposed to provide rooms. If you are assigned to a home, complain to the committee and make them change you two or three times until you find a room that suits you. They will not mind the trouble; that is why they are there, to make you comfortable. If the Board of your state is paying your expenses wholly or in part, have the best of everything, the finest rooms, the most expensive meals. What do you care? Somebody else is paying for it all.

Do not forget to write to the program committee before the convention begins, to inform them that you have a very fine address that you will be glad to deliver some time during the session and that you will sing a solo for them or conduct the song services. They will never know what you can do unless you tell them, Oswald. You may achieve a place on the program by doing this. Some preachers do.

And, Oswald, if Mrs. Oswald is on the program, by all means she must wear at least two bracelets, a sparkling necklace, a long, slinky fur neckpiece, a hat that comes down well over the eyes, and a dress of large figured material which is made with a great deal of trimming. This ensemble will prove to be very fascinating if she wears white gloves also; her white paws waving will further hypnotize the audience.

If you are elected chairman of a convention, be sure that everyone understands clearly every announcement made during the session. To insure this, repeat each announcement after the person making it has finished. Also repeat parts of — and comment on all — statements, discussions, and sermons of the convention. Emphasize every point that you consider worth remembering. This will help your audience to grasp and retain important truths that they might otherwise overlook. Do not be afraid to talk. After all, you were chosen chairman and it is *your* meeting.

It is very odd, Ozzy, but I have so often observed that the preacher who can never stay in one place a year, and who never preaches to over thirty people, will make a great impassioned address on "How to Fill Our Empty

The nearest you got was the keyhole

Pews." And the fellow who has not had a prayer meeting in his church in five years will talk on "How to Conduct a Successful Prayer Meeting."

By all means, when the convention is over and you have returned to your church, preach a sermon to your people, Oswald, taking full credit for every forward movement launched by the convention. Let them know that your ideas and plans were adopted and that you set the whole group right, and that but for you the state program would be a sorry thing indeed. Your people will have no means of discovering that the nearest you got to the Forward Committee's session was just to the keyhole of the room in which they were meeting, and that the only voice you had in the convention was when you timidly piped, "I move we adjourn."

12

The Last Word

There will be that sunny day when you will be forced to sit in your office and listen to Mrs. Weighty tell you why Hortense should be pianist, when Hortense is too slow to catch cold and can't play anything beyond second-grade music.

❀ ❀

Or you must listen to Mr. Shiftless whine because he can't hold a job, when you know and do not dare tell him that he is the laziest man in three counties.

❀ ❀

You will find that ignorance and stupidity are other names for the devil.

❀ ❀

Preachers are the poorest listeners of any class of people in the world. This is probably due to the fact that all of their training and experience have to do with talking, not listening.

❀ ❀

When you are utterly failing at your task and your crowds are dwindling, Oswald, call in an expert. (An expert is any man away from home.) He will be expensive, but it will be well worth it to sustain your reputation and that of the church. Remember, he also must see to his own standing. So do not grumble at his method of getting numbers — or money!

Don't say I didn't warn you

There will be times, Oswald, after business meetings especially, when after weeks of careful planning and prayer, your cherished plans for the good of the most are defeated by an ignorant and indifferent minority who gather bent on mischief, that you will feel like butting out your brains against the barn. It will take Christian grace, Oswald, to remain sweet.

🌹 🌹

When taking collections for special objects or projects, ask your congregation to give fives and tens. You put in a dime. Some preachers do.

🌹 🌹

Have a hobby, Oswald. Keep bees, or make a garden, or raise fishing worms in a tub in the basement — anything to save your reason.

🌹 🌹

It may be your lot to become the pastor of the largest church in a city where are located several churches of your denomination. In that case you will suffer much at the hands of your fellow ministers. They will "pick" at your every work and deed, at your mode of living, your manner of dress, and your children's behavior. Where you would expect to find brotherly co-operation and fellowship, you will often find jealousy and envy.

🌹 🌹

In the course of events, Oswald, there may arise circumstances and conditions that will constitute an emergency which will call for a reduction of the preacher's salary. Now this is the peculiar thing that you will notice: So far as the church and the preacher's salary are concerned, the emergency continues and continues and continues!

Also, Oswald, the church will probably pay first all current bills due, and let you do the waiting. They consider it a disgrace for the church to owe bills in town, but it is never a disgrace to owe the preacher, or for him to go in debt because he is not paid.

Some preachers do!

You may rail at your membership constantly because one or two play an occasional game of bridge; but it is quite different if you, by the hour, engage in golf, or croquet, or horseshoe games and tournaments, thereby neglecting prayer, study, and personal contact on the field with members who need your service. I cannot see the difference, Oswald, frankly.

🌹 🌹

Your people will rise and sing lustily, "Onward, Christian Soldiers, Marching as to War," or "Awake" and then will settle placidly down to gentle slumber during the rest of the service. So much of our Christianity is like that.

🌹 🌹

What grand and glorious victories we would have in our churches if it were not for circumstances and conditions. These two items are responsible for more failures than is Satan, and seem to hold more terrors for preachers and people alike, than hell itself. At least we hear more about them.

🌹 🌹

Just before you go into your pulpit, oh, so often, someone with a grievance or a grouch or a woe will descend upon you and unload. Away will go serenity; away will go peace; away will go sermon; and shattered in heart and nerves you will be expected to go into the service and preach as if nothing had happened. This makes you feel that the more you see of people the better you like goats — which feeling is very good for sermons.

🌹 🌹

Once upon a time, preachers were expected to preach. Today a preacher must be a Big Businessman and a "Go-Getter."

There are churches that expect to keep a preacher only a year or two. They have devised a neat and unique little way to get rid of the minister. They simply starve him out. God help you, if you fall among thieves, Oswald. Some preachers do.

In the pulpit and out, they have to listen

Some neighborhoods, Oswald, are very trying. It may be your misfortune to be domiciled next to one of these tongue-and-eye women. If so, you are lost. You can pull down all your shades, lock your outer doors and at midnight turn out all your lights, retreat to the back bedroom, shut the door, hide under the bed, and sneeze. The next morning she will ask you how your cold is.

🌹 🌹

If you ever, in the course of events, divorce your wife, your preaching will be affected to this extent: you can never mention divorce in the pulpit. If you have one wife in Texas and you are living with another in Ohio, sooner or later the story will follow you. These things have an uncanny way of getting about. You might choose some single issue, Divine Healing, or the Second Coming, and preach so loudly and with such fervor on the subject that no one of your followers will ever think of divorce.

🌹 🌹

When wild oats are being harvested in your membership, you will be expected to assist by helping to hold the bag and by praying for a poor yield.

🌹 🌹

Keep busy! Whether it makes sense or not, do something! A congregation does not appreciate a lazy pastor. It is better to run in circles than to sit still. Anyway, you will have to travel fast to stay *where you are.*

🌹 🌹

A good pastor is one who stays by the church in troubles they would not have had if they had not called him.

🌹 🌹

There are individuals who will not allow you to be pastor of a church, except in name only. Mr. Dom N. Ear,

Mr. Money-Bags, and Mr. Bust M. Up will constitute a committee to see that you do not have too much authority. They will plan for you and be your spokesmen. They run the church and the pastor — otherwise the pastor must *go* — and some preachers do!

🌹 🌹

"Saved to Serve" means with some people "saved to serve dinners and to work in the Ladies' Aid." They will expect you to line up with this unscriptural method of raising money, Oswald, and will probably ask you to sell fancy work or food in stands at picnics or fairs and to sell chances on quilts, all of which is done in the name of the church, in order to raise money to pay the bills of the church. Your wife will have to make chili and pies and wash dishes to earn money to pay your salary. To protest is to bring trouble upon yourself. You may try it, though. Some preachers do.

🌹 🌹

It is better, Oswald, to suffer your right arm to be cut off than for you to be the cause of a church split. A church split is a tragedy pure and simple. If you can't hold your congregation together, get out and let some other man have a try. Really, there are some men who can do it, believe it or not!

🌹 🌹

Never think that you have all the truth. Do not be guilty of possessing the obsession that no man is left to preach the truth but yourself. And all men who disagree with you are not wrong, Ozzie.

Preachers love audiences. They grow so accustomed to them and to speechmaking that they often seem to carry about an invisible audience to admire and to applaud. Preachers' wives listen to more speeches than any class of people in this world. They listen to their husbands, in the pulpit and out; they hear sermons and addresses rehearsed over the dishes, the mending, the ironing, and during the meals. Preachers become so accustomed to presiding and preaching that they unconsciously carry pulpit habits into situations where they do not best suit. For instance, I have seen a preacher monopolize a whole dinner party for hours, relating his own experiences and opinions. Since you are Emma Alice's son, you will probably be this type. The only advantage that the radio has over Emma Alice is that you can shut a radio off. You may have acquired some of her habits of speech. When some long-suffering dinner partner bashes you over the head and quietly takes his departure, don't say I didn't warn you.

🌼 🌼

Stand up and yell for what you want in life, Oswald. Some preachers do! This little rhyme will help you to remember:

> Yell loud and long
> And do not cease;
> The squeaking wheel
> Will get the grease.

🌼 🌼

There is no preacher so miserable as the man who is too big for a little place and too little for a big place.

There are people who disapprove of smoking. If you smoke, keep right on. Doubtless you can hide the fact from your congregation. Some preachers do.

If there are grocers who are members of your church, drop into their stores and help yourself. They will not mind at all if you dip into their cookies, their meat, and their cheese and crackers. Calmly appropriate a pint of milk each morning and drink it. Never offer to pay for any of this.

Have your wife ordained, Oswald. Then she can ride on clergy fare and in your absence, she can perform the wedding ceremonies, and collect the fees.

There are two priceless possessions that a preacher may have, Oswald. The first is tact. The second is a sense of humor. These will serve you when reason and logic fail.

A preacher's table manners are very important; allow me to give you a few helpful hints. In order to put your hosts at ease, when offered a napkin you can refuse it with a grand gesture — "We won't need those — let's do away with style." Or accept it and tuck it under your chin. Eat noisily and greedily, holding your fork as if it were a shovel. Peas and similar foods can be eaten with a knife. Some preachers do!

There are two overworked expressions in the preacher's vocabulary. The word "great" is one, Oswald, and the phrase, "since I came here," is the other. Read the reports from the churches in your denominational paper and see how often these are used! Learn some new adjectives and forget "since I came here."

🌹 🌹

Those who climb to the very top, Oswald, often find that it is rough going and that the wind is in their faces. To go high will mean sacrifice and hard work, and faithfulness to an ideal, and loneliness. In the ministry as in other walks of life, there are many who are common and few who are uncommon. An uncommon man is rarely understood or forgiven by the common mass.

> He who climbs to mountain peak
>   Must stand amid the thunder,
> Beside the lightning's forked tongue
>   And boulders split asunder.
>
> He who climbs to mountain peak
>   A fine strength spends;
> His shivering spirit stands alone,
>   In high cold winds.
>
> But he who climbs to mountain peak
>   May see afar;
> May reach a trembling, eager hand
>   To touch a star.

🌹 🌹

You may not like many things I have said to you, Oswald, in this little book. But remember, Ozzy, my boy, that the hit dog howls. The hit dog howls!